THE INCARNATION

As a Layman Sees It

> The humanity of the Son of God is everything to us. It is the golden chain that binds our souls to Christ, and through Christ to God. This is to be our study. Christ was a real man..." The Youth's Instructor, October 13, 1898.

> For innumerable evils have compassed me about: mine iniquities have taken hold upon me, so that I am not able to look up, they are more than the hairs of mine head: therefore my heart faileth me." Psalms 40:12

> I am weary of my crying: my throat is dried : mine eyes fail while I wait for my God. O God, thou knowest my foolishness; and my sins are not hid from thee." Psalms 69:3,5

Richard Allen Waterman, Jr.
February 1979
Revised March 2022

INTRODUCTION

Only a newcomer to the faith or someone who does not involve himself in doctrinal discussion would say that there is no controversy in the church over the subject of the nature of Christ.   This paper is not presented to add controversy; but, rather, it is the author's hope it might help in some small way to solve the confused concepts now existing within our ranks.

I do not believe there should be any confusion about the nature of Christ, nor do I believe that we will spend eternity trying to ascertain whether or not Christ took sinful flesh, or sinless flesh. I think the Bible and the Spirit of Prophecy are very clear on this point. God became a real man, and eternity is too short to fully comprehend the condescension. How did God become man? No one knows, but He did become man, and I know by experience what man is. Therefore, there should be no confusion as to what He became. It is how He became man that causes us to stand baffled before the Godhead. This paper deals with the what and not the how.   Please do not look for perfection in this thought paper.   I only ask that you read it prayerfully and critically with an open mind. I will accept opposing views and will study the same with an open mind.

Richard A. Waterman
8 MacMillan Drive
Brunswick, ME 04011
Telephone: 207-725-4750

Note from the author:

As you can see, this is a study I put together over 43 years ago. After reviewing it recently for consideration for our Church web site, I chose not to edit it in any way, even though I could have condensed it considerably. Let me say though, I have not changed my views one iota. As a matter of fact, the views I have set forth in this study have been reinforced by authors such as J.R Zurcher in his book, "Touched with Our Feelings." Review and Herald, 1999. (See Kenneth Wood's statement on page 19 of the preface and also a statement on page 259 released by the E.G. White Estate where Sister White states that Christ was "subjected to all the evil tendencies which man is heir." This statement can also be found in the Adventist Review, February 17, 1994. Also see Ralph Larson's book, "The Word Was Made Flesh," Cherrystone Press, 1986, Cherry Valley, California. In it are found over 1200 statements from Adventist pioneers and publications that I believe affirm the position I have taken in my study.

Although, in retrospect, much more could have been added to this study, the point that I wanted to convey, I feel I have accomplished.

I want to thank my wife, Donna, for her many hours of typing and research, without which this work would have not been accomplished.

I would also like to thank H.J. Emerson for editing and preparing this paper for publication. H.J. Emerson's theological publications can be found through Amazon.com.

Where does one begin on such an important subject as the nature of Christ? Since my primary source of information for this study is the Spirit of Prophecy, let me introduce a quote found in the Review and Herald, April 5, 1906:

"That God should thus be manifest in the flesh, is indeed a mystery; and without the help of the Holy Spirit, we cannot hope to comprehend this subject. The most humbling lesson that man has to learn is the nothingness of human wisdom, and the folly of trying, by his own unaided efforts, to find out God."

Should we involve ourselves in the study of the nature of Christ? Again, I quote Mrs. White:

"The humanity of the Son of God is everything to us…This is to be our study. Christ was a real man…We should come to this study with the humility of a learner, with a contrite heart. And the study of the incarnation of Christ is a fruitful field, which will repay the searcher who digs deep for hidden truth." The Youth's Instructor. October 13, 1898.

Mrs. White never discouraged the study of the nature of Christ, as you can see in the statement just quoted, although we are cautioned that we should not dwell upon these subjects. I perceive that there is danger in approaching subjects which dwell on the humanity of the Son of the Infinite God." ---S.D.A. Commentary, Vol. 5, page 1129.

He was also divine. We should present a balanced picture of Christ.

Before I go any further, I would like to state very briefly my views on the nature of Christ. I believe that on His divine side, He was truly God, and on His human side, He was truly man. He existed from all eternity, and He was equal with the Father in all respects. It was His choice to come to this earth and be born of His virgin mother, Mary, and inherit from her just what every other child inherits, namely sinful flesh, or a "degraded" "fallen nature" "defiled by sin."

I cannot accept the concept that He inherited a sinless nature. This is the Catholic concept which should not be entertained by any serious Bible scholar. He was not exempt from the law of heredity. We are told in Desire of Ages, page 49, that He accepted it. Jesus Christ was born born-again, by that I mean that the Holy Spirit was in the mind of Christ the very moment of birth. But this does not mean that He did not take a sinful nature.

You might liken this experience to that of a diabetic. He is sustained daily by insulin; his body is still that of a diabetic. This is much the same as the Christian who is sustained daily by the Holy Spirit; yet, he, too, retains the corrupt flesh. Although He took a sinful nature, at no time in His life did the sinful nature ever become the dominating factor in His life. In his flesh, not in His mind, but in His flesh He felt the pressures of all the impulses and tendencies wherewith man is beset.

These tendencies which were in His flesh were continually striving or "clamoring" for indulgence just as they are in all human beings, the one difference being Christ never submitted to these inclinations of the flesh. Therefore, Christ was not only my substitute but He was my example in all things. He was tempted in all points, inwardly and outwardly, as all human beings are tempted. This is the inspired position of the Bible and the premise of this thought paper.

Why is it so important for us to understand whether or not Christ took a sinful nature or a sinless nature? It is very important because, as I said in the previous statement, Christ is not only my substitute, He is my example. Now if Christ did not take a sinful nature, then He could not be tempted in all points as man is tempted.

Temptation is not merely an external matter. All sinful promptings must pass through the mind for acceptance or rejection which necessarily makes all temptation an internal matter, whether the promptings come from the law in "my members" or an external source.

The nature that Christ assumed was an integral part of the message of righteousness by faith presented at the 1888 Conference by Jones and Waggoner. Jones was very strong in his presentation of the nature of Christ; that is, that Christ, on the human side, had precisely our nature, the nature of the seed of Abraham which extends back to Adam. Jones' viewpoint can be clearly seen in his sermons given at the 1895 General Conference which have been reproduced in the book The Third Angel's Message, Sermons Given at the General Conference of 1895. Even though Jones presented his viewpoint very strongly, nowhere in the writings of the Spirit of Prophecy do you find Mrs. White ever condemning Jones for his view on this subject. Yet, she was very quick to condemn the views of Kellogg in his book, The Living Temple. I believe she would have done the same thing with Jones and Waggoner had they been presenting heresy, as Kellogg was.

Selected Messages, Book One, page 378, "you look in reality upon these subjects as I do." It was not what he presented, but how he presented it, that led Mrs. White to caution him.

Now because of Jones and Wagoner's position, there were many who started writing to Mrs. White about this subject of the nature of Christ. To these inquiries, she replied: "Letters have been coming to me, affirming that Christ could not have had the same nature as man, for if He had, He would have fallen under similar temptations. If He did not have man's nature, He could not be our example.

If He was not a partaker of our nature; He could not have been tempted as man has been. If it were not possible for Him to yield to temptation, He could not be our helper. It was a solemn reality that Christ came to fight the battles as man, in man's behalf. His temptation and victory tell us that humanity must copy the Pattern; man must become a partaker of the divine nature. Selected Messages, Book One, page 408.

The people writing the letters were saying that Christ could not have taken the sinful nature. Mrs. White says just the opposite, doesn't she?

Let me quote a couple of statements from the Spirit of Prophecy in regard to the nature of Christ, as far as the sinful nature is concerned:

"He took upon His sinless nature, our sinful nature that He might know how to succor those that are tempted." Medical Ministry, page 181.

Again, in Review and Herald, December 15, 1896:

"Clad in the vestments of humanity, the Son of God came down to the level of those He wished to save. In Him was no guile or sinfulness; He was ever pure and undefiled; yet He took upon Him our sinful nature."

Now notice, "in Him" was no guile or sinfulness. You see, she must mean that in the mind of Christ, as far as His character was concerned, as far as His attitude was concerned, there was no sin of His own. Yet, the nature that He assumed had in it all the sin that every human being inherits at birth. We must take these statements and look at them closely and not read anything into them, and on the other hand, do not take anything from them.

I think right here I would like to state that one of the reasons why we have so much confusion in the church today on this subject is that we fail to make the distinction between the higher and lower nature. I believe that the higher nature must control the lower nature at all times. Now when I say higher nature, I mean that, by faith, we reach out and receive the mind of Christ. That mind that we receive by faith must ever be in control. Never should we allow the flesh to take command and control us. The Spirit of Prophecy is very clear that man is made up of a higher nature and a lower nature.

I'm not going to take the time to quote a lot of statements, although there are many that could be presented: but rather, I'll use just this one found in Prophets and Kings, page 489:

"The tendencies of the physical nature, unless under the dominion of a higher power, will surely work ruin and death. The body is to be brought into subjection to the higher powers of the being. The passions are to be controlled by the will, which is itself to be under the control of God. The kingly power of reason, sanctified by divine grace, is to bear sway in the life."

Now I think that statement is about as good a statement as can be found in the Spirit of Prophecy on that subject. Like I say there are many more, but I will not take time now to present them here.

I think this thought is presented by Paul in Romans 7:21-23 where he says, "I delight in the law of God after the inward man: but I see another law in my members, warring against the law of my mind, and bringing me into captivity to the law of sin which is in my members." Now notice, he saw this law of sin in his members, but he recognized another law in his mind. He saw that these two laws were in conflict, the law of sin in his flesh and the law of God in the mind. Again, this is only one statement that can be taken from the Bible. There are many more like it, but I think this text points out what I'm trying to say.

Now here I want to introduce another thought found in Adventist Home, page 127:

"The lower passions have their seat in the body and work through it. The words "flesh" or "fleshly" or "carnal lusts" embrace the lower, corrupt nature; the flesh of itself cannot act contrary to the will of God."

Let's analyze this. There are passions and lust in the flesh according to the Spirit of Prophecy, but these things which are in our flesh cannot act contrary to the will of God. They must find a response in the mind. I think this is well stated in Testimonies, Vol. 5, page 177:

"Guile includes impurity in all its forms. An impure thought tolerated, an unholy desire cherished, and the soul is contaminated, its integrity compromised. Then when lust hath conceived, it bringeth forth sin; and sin when it is finished, bringeth forth death."

Now notice, the lust must be conceived before it brings forth sin. In other words, there will be temptations to lust in the flesh, but as long as they remain in the flesh, and you are not submitting to them and allowing them to become a dominating factor in your life, you are not considered an active sinner. Therefore, it was the same with Christ; He never submitted to lustful temptations, but at the same time it can be said that He took a sinful nature. His flesh was filled with these hereditary seeds of disobedience, but they remained in the flesh. At no time did they become a part of His mind by choice.

Mrs. White continues:

"If we would not commit sin, we must shun its very beginnings. Every emotion and desire must be held in subjection to reason and conscience. Every unholy thought must be instantly repelled." Ibid.

Now notice, it is possible to be tempted by an unholy thought, but it must be instantly repelled. If you instantly repel it, then you are not held accountable for it. Likewise, Christ could have been tempted by a sinful thought, but He instantly repelled it; so, therefore, He never sinned in thought, deed, or word. That's how you put the two together. He never sinned in thought, yet a sinful thought crossed His mind, but He did not cherish that thought. Therefore, He was not considered a sinner.

"To your closet, followers of Christ. Pray in faith and with all the heart. Satan is watching to ensnare your feet. You must have help from above if you would escape his devices. By faith and prayer all may meet the requirements of the gospel. No man can be forced to transgress. His own consent must be first gained; the soul must purpose the sinful act before passion can dominate over reason or iniquity triumph over conscience. Temptation, however strong, is never an excuse for sin." Ibid.

Now how long will this battle go on? According to the Spirit of Prophecy, Testimonies, Vol. 4, page 439, it states:

"Meditate seriously upon these things, and then in the fear of God gird on the armor for a life conflict with hereditary tendencies, imitating none but the divine Pattern."

"Self, self, will be continually active for recognition, even in the very holiest of exercises. MS 182, 1903, found in "In Heavenly Places", page 220.

Now I ask you how could we imitate Christ in striving against these hereditary tendencies if Christ was never tempted by any of these hereditary tendencies?

Here is a statement from the SDA Bible Commentary, Vol., 4, page 1147, from E G. White.

"He took upon Himself fallen, suffering human nature, degraded and defiled by sin."

Again, SDA Bible Commentary, Vol.5, page 1131, she makes this statement:

"In taking upon Himself man's nature in fallen condition, Christ did not in the least participates in its sin."

Brothers and sisters, we need to look at this statement closely and not add anything to it. Christ did not in the least participate in its sin. Now Mrs. White does not say that Christ inherited a nature without sin in it. She's not saying that; but, rather, "its" is referring back to the nature which He took. It does not say He did not participate in man's sinful nature; but, rather, He did not participate in its sin. So let us put it this way: Christ inherited the sinful nature of man, but He did not participate in the sin that was in that nature. That's how that statement should be understood.

Another statement found in Special Instruction Relating to the Review and Herald Office and the Work of Battle Creek, May 31, 1896, page 13:

"Though He had no taint of sin upon His character, yet He condescended to connect our fallen human nature with His divinity."

Now notice, there was not a taint of sin upon His character, or His mind, but at the same time, He took the sinful nature. Mrs. White says:

"The Christian will feel the promptings of sin, for the flesh lusteth against the Spirit; but the Spirit striveth against the flesh, keeping up a constant warfare".

Here is where Christ's help is needed. Human weakness becomes united to divine strength, and faith exclaims, "Thanks be to God, which giveth us the victory through our Lord Jesus Christ" (1Cor.15:57) The Sanctified Life, 1937 Edition, page 66.

Notice the word "constant" and also notice that a Christian will feel the promptings of sin. That does not mean that he is an active sinner just because these promptings are coming at him. He must give in to the promptings. There must be a constant warfare against these things. "Thanks be to God, which gives us the victory."

How can Christ give us the victory over that which He did not gain the victory? He couldn't; therefore, He had to be tempted in all points as I am tempted in order to give me the victory over all the points that I am tempted in. Thank God that He did gain the victory.

How could Christ come down to this earth and take upon Himself human nature "degraded and defiled by sin" and yet live a sinless life? That is a mystery. There would be no mystery for Christ to come down and take a sinless nature like angels. I see nothing mysterious about that at all; but, thank God, He did not come down as an angel.

He became man, and He lived the life of man, and I praise His holy name for it, although I cannot fully comprehend how He could do it.

What are some of the problems that are involved when we accept the concept that Christ inherited a sinless nature? Number one is that He is not my example.

Number two is, since He is not my example in all things, I will enter into (subconsciously maybe) a counterfeit righteousness by faith. That is, since Christ is not my example in all things and merely my substitute, then I will enter into righteousness by subsidy. In other words, I'll do my best and Christ will make up the difference. It is very dangerous to accept the concept that Christ inherited a sinless nature. Let us not enter into that fatal deception of the devil.

Mrs. White says, "When we see the length of the chain that was let down for us, when we understand something of the infinite sacrifice Christ has made in our behalf, the heart is melted with tenderness and contrition." --Steps to Christ, page 36. I would like to submit that if we take one of the links out of that chain, whether it be the top link which would destroy His divinity or the bottom link which would destroy His complete humanity, we have destroyed the plan of salvation. He was totally divine. He was totally human aside from sinning.

Let's look at the construction of the sanctuary for a minute. Remember the tent itself, the tabernacle, was made from dried skins of animals, but within those dead skins dwelt the Shekinah glory, the very presence of God. Our flesh, "sinful," "degraded," and "defiled by sin," which Mrs. White also refers to as a "casket," will become the dwelling place of that

Shekinah glory again, if we will allow it. I believe that those dead animal skins were a symbol of the sinful flesh of man; yet, God in His love will dwell within that sinful flesh. The floor of the tabernacle was made of dirt, to me, symbolizing the fact that Christ came all the way down to the earth; He met man at man's lowest level. Herein is the beauty and love of Christ.

If we remove the bottom link whereby we destroy the complete humanity of Christ, we might as well become Catholics today because the Priesthood of Catholicism is based on the concept that Christ did not inherit a sinful nature; but rather, a sinless nature from His sinless mother. If He did not inherit a sinful nature, He could not identify totally with humanity and could not have become the connecting link between divinity and humanity. The priesthood was set up to be that connecting link, linking sinful humanity with a sinless Christ. The priesthood becomes the bottom link; and, thereby, wrongfully assumes the prerogative of Christ. A Christ with a sinless nature cannot connect fallen humanity with divinity because He, like the angels, would not know by experience what fallen man must go through. In the Catholic Church, sinful man is not only required to make confession to the priest but also ask for the intercession of Mary, the Saints, and Jesus Christ. There are many links between God and man in the Catholic Church, but we are told in Acts 4:12 that there "is none other name under heaven given among men whereby we must be saved."

The reason why the Catholic Church cannot accept a Christ who took a sinful nature is that they believe in the doctrine of original sin, which means that one who is born with a sinful nature is a sinner. This I do not believe. We, like David, are conceived in sin, but we are not born active sinners. There is a difference. Sin is either an overt act or an inward desire. Babies are not born in a state of active sin. If we believe so, then why don't we baptize our babies, as the Catholic Church does?

For an excellent explanation of this subject (original sin), I refer you to the article in the Review and Herald, September 23, 1965, entitled," What About 'Original Sin? See appendix A. That is one of the best articles I have ever read on this subject. That is the position I hold, and I believe it is the historic position of this church.

As far as children being born sinners, let's look at this statement found in Patriarchs and Prophets, page 306:

"It is inevitable that children should suffer from the consequences of parental wrongdoing, but they are not punished for the parents' guilt, except as they participate in their sins. It is usually the case, however, that children walk in the steps of their parents. By inheritance and example, the sons become partakers of the father's sin. Wrong tendencies, perverted appetites, and debased morals, as well as physical disease and degeneracy, are transmitted as the legacy from father to son, to the third and fourth generation. This fearful truth should have solemn power to restrain men from following a course of sin."

Notice that the children are not punished, nor are they held accountable, for their parents' sins. Even though these tendencies are transmitted to their children, the children must act upon these tendencies, I think this statement, if looked at and studied, will prove my point, that we are not born active sinners; but rather, we are born in sin with the capacity, with a bent, with a natural tendency toward it. If we are not born again, we will continually act upon these tendencies and continually sin. There is nothing else that man can do but sin without the aid of the Holy Spirit. That's why we must be born again. When we are born again, the Holy Spirit will work in us against these tendencies, as He did in Christ. Then we fight the battle as He fought the battle. There will be the clamoring, the tendencies, the promptings, but we will have the victory over them in Christ Jesus.

I want to submit right here that I do not believe that because a person is not born a sinner that he has any strength or any power in himself that can stop him from sinning. It's impossible. He will sin automatically at three months, four years, I don't know when God would consider one a sinner. I'm not about to set any specific age, all I know is that it must be an intelligent choice. We are told in Scripture, "Therefore to him that knoweth to do good, and doeth it not, to him it is a sin." James 4:17. So one must have an understanding of right and wrong before one is held accountable for his sin.

When a person is born again, does he lose the sinful nature. No. We are told: "...for the fallen nature of Adam always strives for the mastery." --Adventist Home, page 205

Notice, that fallen nature always strives. Now in order for it to strive always, it's always got to be with us. Likewise, it must have been with Christ also.

"They (passions) will clamor for indulgence..." Gospel Workers, page 128.

"There is wrestling with inbred sin. There is warfare against outward wrong." Review and Herald, November 29, 1887.

"We must strive daily against outward evil and inward sin if we would reach perfection of Christian character. Review and Herald, May 30, 1882.

"None of the apostles and prophets ever claimed to be without sin. Men who have lived the nearest to God, men who would sacrifice life itself rather than knowingly commit a wrong act, men whom God has honored with divine light and power, have confessed the sinfulness of their nature. They have put no confidence in the flesh, have claimed no righteousness of their own, but have trusted wholly in the righteousness of Christ."   Acts of the Apostles, page 561

Let's look at that statement closely. Notice, these apostles, who were living the nearest to God, would rather die than knowingly commit a wrong act, but yet, they still confessed that they had a sinful nature. I think that it is one of the clearest statements in the Spirit of Prophecy showing us that the sinful nature will remain with us right up until the time Christ comes.   So, if we must overcome as Christ overcame, then He had to overcome the same way I have to overcome.   He had to deal with the same nature that I have to deal with.   If He was not tempted exactly as I am, inwardly and outwardly, then He was not tempted in all points; and, therefore, the devil could shout, "Foul," and you had better believe he would have shouted loud and clear.

It was a solemn reality that Jesus overcame as I must overcome.

You see, if Christ had inherited a different flesh from what I inherit, then He would have had holy flesh. Right? But, is it right to say that in this life men can have holy flesh? No. Sister White says in Book Two of Selected Messages, page 33

"When human beings receive holy flesh, they will not remain on the earth, but will be taken to heaven. While sin is forgiven in this life, its results are not now wholly removed. It is at His coming that Christ is to 'change our vile body, that it may be fashioned like unto his glorious body." (Phil. 3:21)

Now notice, we will have vile body right up until the time Christ comes. Remember, Christ overcame in the same flesh in which we must overcome.

Now let's take two statements from the Spirit of prophecy and put them together. The first one is found in Vol. 6 of the SDA Bible Commentary, page 1118:

"Those only who through faith in Christ obey all of God's commandments will reach this condition of sinlessness in which Adam lived before his transgression. They testify to their love of Christ by obeying all His precepts (MS 122, 1901)."

The second statement is found in the Signs of the Times, March 23, 1888:

"We cannot say, 'I am sinless," till this vile body is changed and fashioned like unto His glorious body."

Now how do you put the two together? We are told in one place that only those who through faith keep all the commandments of God will reach the state of sinlessness; and, yet, she says we cannot say that we are sinless until the vile body is changed. Is Mrs. White a schizophrenic? Does she contradict herself? Of course not, we should understand it this way. We will be transformed by the renewing of our minds; but we will retain the sinful flesh, the sinful, vile, corrupt body, right up to the time of translation.

"Behold, I shew you a mystery; We shall not all sleep, but we shall all be changed, in a moment, in the twinkling of an eye, at the last trump; for the trumpet shall sound, and the dead shall be raised incorruptible, and we shall be changed. For this corruptible must put on incorruption, and this mortal must but on immortality."—1 Cor. 15:51-53.

The sinless nature concept is the basis of the heresy that evolved within our own church between the years 1901 and 1903 in the Indiana Conference. We must reject any doctrine that would teach that we must receive holy flesh before Christ comes. Sister White says, "It is an impossibility." Not a soul of you has holy flesh now" "It is an impossibility" although she says "all may now obtain holy hearts." "While we cannot claim perfection of the flesh, we may have Christian perfection of the soul."- Selected Messages, Book 2, page 32.

Again, do you see how vital it is that we make the distinction between the mind and the body, or the mind and the flesh? If we don't make that distinction, we are going to be in constant controversy.

You may be asking yourself the question," Does he believe in the holistic concept?"

Most definitely, I do. I believe that our sinful members still can be set aside for a holy purpose. I do not believe that sin will be put out of the flesh in this life, but I do believe that God will take even sinful flesh and use it to His glory. He will not use a sinful mind to His glory, but He will come in and dwell within sinful flesh and use these members to His glory. So, in that sense our members are to be sanctified. Sanctified, to me, means to be set-aside for a holy purpose, in some cases. In other cases, sanctified means to be made holy. Still, in other cases, it means both, such as the Sabbath. I believe we are to have holy minds, sinless minds. I believe our members, even though they are sinful, are also to be sanctified (set apart for a holy purpose). We can use the word both ways.

Sister White does so repeatedly. Another reason why I feel there is a lot of confusion on the subject of the nature of Christ, is that some of us approach it from a subjective standpoint. We lift out one statement here or there from the Spirit of Prophecy or the Bible, and we base our conclusion on that one text, or possibly two, which justify our own preconceived opinions. I believe the only way we can ever reach an intelligent conclusion is to study everything that is available to us, taking all sixty-six books of the Bible and the Spirit of Prophecy into consideration.

The use of this subjective approach results in the multiplicity of denominations and beliefs. For an example: Paul says in Romans 2:13, "For not the hearers of the law are just before God, but the doers of the law shall be justified." Then in Romans 3:20, he says, "Therefore by the deeds of the law there shall no flesh be justified in his sight: for by the law is the knowledge of sin." One place he says the doers of the law shall be justified and another he says by the deeds of the law no flesh shall be justified. One person could take the statement in Romans 2:13 and very dogmatically present his view.

The other person could come at it from Romans 3:20 and, just as dogmatically, present his position. I believe that this has too often been our approach on the subject of the nature of Christ. I do not believe that this is the correct way. We need to bring in the third text and balance the other two. What it means to be a doer of the law will solve the issue between Romans 2:13 and 3:20. By receiving Jesus Christ by faith the righteousness which the law demands is fulfilled in us, Romans 8:4. So, by taking Romans 8:4 and bringing it in with these other two texts, the problem is solved. So, again, I urge that whenever you approach any subject, take all the writings into consideration before you defend, or present a doctrine or a position.

The following statement found in Great Controversy, page 473, used to bother me a bit until I balanced it with a statement found in 2 Selected Messages, page 32:

"The sanctification set forth in the Scriptures embraces the entire being—spirit, soul, and body. Paul prayed for the Thessalonians that their 'whole spirit and soul and body be preserved blameless unto the coming of our Lord Jesus Christ.' 1 Thessalonians 5:23."

At first, this statement seemed to be saying that we must have holy flesh, but in 2 Selected Messages, page 32, she says it's an impossibility.

At this point, the thought crossed my mind that maybe there is such a thing as holy flesh, not like the flesh that they were trying to obtain in the Indiana Holy Flesh Movement, but somehow the flesh through grace was holy. My confusion was cleared up when I read this statement:

"The Scriptures teach us to seek for the sanctification to God of body, soul, and spirit. In this work we are to be laborers together with God. Much may be done to restore the moral image of God in man, to improve the physical, mental, and moral capabilities. Great changes can be made in the physical system by obeying the laws of God and bringing into the body nothing that defiles. And while we cannot claim perfection of the flesh, we may have Christian perfection of the soul." 2 Selected Messages, page 32.

Many other statements could be brought in at this point to support the fact that we will not receive holy flesh until Christ returns, but I want to devote the rest of this thought paper to an explanation of the statements relating to the nature of Christ found in the Appendix of Vol. 7A of the SDA Bible Commentary.

Explanations of Statements Found in the Appendix of Questions on Doctrine or The Appendix of Volume 7A of the SDA Bible Commentary Prefaced by a brief comment on the historic concept of the nature of Christ. All emphasis in this and the preceding section is that of the author.

While I strongly recommend the book, Vol. 7A, I do not recommend Questions on Doctrine, especially when it comes to the subject of the nature of Christ or the atonement.

Questions on Doctrine is the result of the Barnhouse-Martin meetings with the General Conference brethren back in the early 1950's (See the Introduction on page 7). I believe there were some compromises made with the Evangelicals, compromises which do not harmonize with the historical position of this church. Right here I would like to introduce a statement by Kenneth Wood, Editor of Review and Herald:

"Some believe that Jesus, as a true human being, accepted the same kind of genetic disadvantages that all others born into this world must accept. The Sabbath school lessons * take this view which was the view set forth in all Adventist literature until recent times. Others argue that, if Christ had taken human nature 'with all its liabilities' (Desire of Ages, page 117, He would have been a sinner Himself in need of a Savior. They emphasize that Christ being the second Adam took the same nature Adam possessed in his pre-fall condition.

Ellen G. White points out, of course, that the flesh cannot of itself act contrary to the will of God.' In Heavenly Places, page 198. It is neutral, performing only those acts to which the mind gives consent.... (* "Jesus the Model Man," Second Quarter, 1977, H.E. Douglass.)

And perhaps one reason is that for a number of years too many members and ministers have feared to discuss the humanity of Christ lest they appear irreverent and seem to make Christ 'altogether human' (which He was not; He was also divine). They have been disturbed when some church members and leaders have preached the Christ of historic Adventism, the Christ who lived as we must live, who was tempted as we are tempted, who overcame as we must overcome, and who has promised to live in us by His Holy Spirit..."—Review and Herald, May 5, 1977, page 12.

Some of us believe that "recent times" refers to the 1950's with the Barnhouse—Martin meetings. I would be interested in Mr. Wood's definition of "recent times," One of the first changes I have seen is in "Bible Readings." (See Appendix B) On page 174 of the 1916 edition you will find the statement, "Christ partook of our sinful nature." This statement has been taken out of the later editions. Why? By whom? I believe it is time for the leadership to give an answer to its constituency not only for the changes in Bible Readings but Questions on Doctrine as well.

Now let us look at the statements that are found in the Appendix of these books. I will not be commenting on all of them, but, rather, the ones that I feel have been misused or misunderstood.

Statement No. 1 is found in the Youth Instructor, October 13, 1898. I have quoted a portion of this before, but there are a few things in that statement I wish to comment on again. **She says "the humanity of the Son of God is everything to us. This is to be our study. Christ was a real man... We should come to this study with the humility of a learner...And the study of the incarnation of Christ is a fruitful field which will repay the searcher who digs deep for hidden truth." 7A, p.443, QOD, page 647. Again, she does not discourage the study of the subject; but rather she encourages it.**

"In contemplating the incarnation of Christ in humanity, we stand baffled before an unfathomable mystery, that the human mind cannot comprehend." The Signs of the Times, 7A p. 443, QOD p. 647

Is Mrs. White saying that we cannot understand the type of nature that Christ assumed? No, she is not. She is saying that the incarnation is an unfathomable mystery. I cannot understand or explain how God could become man. No one can, but again, she is not talking about the nature he assumed; but rather how He assumed that nature. How? not, what? is the mystery.

"Was the human nature of the Son of Mary changed into the divine nature of the Son of God? No, the two natures were mysteriously blended in one person-the man Christ Jesus. In Him dwelt all the fullness of the Godhead bodily...7A p. 444 QOD p. 648

This is a great mystery, a mystery that will not be fully, completely understood in all its greatness until the translation of the redeemed shall take place... But the enemy is determined that this gift shall be so mystified that it will become as nothingness" The SDA Bible Commentary, Vol 5, page 1113.

You see, the devil would like to so mystify this subject of the nature of Christ and the incarnation that eventually people will just say, "Well, it's just semantics, why even bother to discuss it. I don't believe that it's essential for salvation, etc." My dear brothers and sisters, it is essential to your salvation.   If you do not understand what Christ became, you cannot possibly understand what you can and must become. It is as simple as that. And if you do not understand what you must become, you will not be ready when Jesus comes.

"...Christ came to the world and suffered all our temptations, and carried all our griefs." Review and Herald, October 1, 1889.

He came to stand at the head of the fallen race, to share in their experience from childhood to manhood. That human beings might be partakers of the divine nature, He came to this earth, and lived a life of perfect obedience," —Review and Herald, June 15, 1905. (7A p. 445 QOD p. 649)

Notice that she says His experience was from childhood to manhood. He was not just tempted in the wilderness; He was tempted all the way from childhood to the Cross.

"The prince of this world came to Christ after His long fast, when He was an hungered, and suggested to Him to command the stones to become bread. But the plan of God, devised for the salvation of man, provided that Christ should know hunger, and poverty, and every phase of man's experience." Review and Herald, Feb 18, 1896. (7A p. 445 QOD p. 649)

"No one, looking upon the childlike countenance shining with animation, could say that Christ was just like other children. He was God in human flesh. when urged by His companions to do wrong, divinity flashed through humanity, and He refused decidedly. In a moment He distinguished between right and wrong, and placed sin in the light of God's commands, holding up the law as a mirror which reflected light upon wrong." — Youth Instructor, Sept.8, 1898. (7A p 445 QOD p. 649

Is Mrs. White saying that Christ did not share in the experience, as all other children do? No. What she is saying is there was something different about His character. He decidedly stood for right. Why? It is because He was born filled with the Holy Ghost. And since He was born filled with the Holy Ghost, he was different. He did act differently. He did respond differently to sin. That does not mean that He had an advantage that we cannot have. According to Sister White, it's possible for our own children to be born filled with the Holy Spirit.

"Even the babe in its mother's arms may dwell as under the shadow of the Almighty through the faith of the praying mother. John the Baptist was filled with the Holy Spirit from his birth. If we will live in communion with God, we too may expect the divine Spirit to mold our little ones, even from their earliest moments." — Desire of Ages, page 512.

So, you see it is possible for us to have children that are born filled with the Holy Ghost.

The next section I would like to deal with is the section entitled, "Took Sinless Human Nature," Section III, in the back of Vol 7A, page 446. Let's consider the bold black heading for a second. I've mentioned this before, but I want to reiterate that this heading is not inspired. It is not from the pen of Mrs. White; but, rather, this is man's opinion. I feel that when one reads this heading, he might possibly be deceived into thinking that the statements that follow will prove such a view. I do not believe the statements that follow prove that Christ took a sinless nature at all, and I will endeavor to prove that they do not.

Another thing I would like to have you consider is that in each statement you will find certain words emphasized. The emphasis is not the emphasis of Mrs. White; but, rather, the emphasis is of man. So, one needs to be very careful as he reads these statements, careful not to read something into them. Use same caution with my underlining, as well. So, with this thought in mind, let's proceed with this section.

"Christ came to the earth, taking humanity and standing as man's representative, to show in the controversy with Satan that man, as God created him, connected with the Father and the Son, could obey every divine requirement." — The Signs of the Times, June 9, 1898.

Notice "as God created him" is emphasized. I believe, with this emphasis, that the authors would have you believe that Christ and Adam were identical as far as their nature is concerned, but this is not so. Jesus Christ was pure; He never sinned. He had a perfect, holy mind - perfect in the sense that He had never sinned, not perfect physically. Adam had a perfect mind, physically and spiritually, and he had a

perfect physical body. Adam was totally perfect, but Jesus Christ was not. Although He had a sinless mind, He did not have sinless flesh. So, the Son of God stood as a human being, as God created us. As He created us human beings, that is the nature Jesus Christ overcame sin with —a human nature - but it was not as strong as the first Adam.
"It was possible for Adam, before the fall, to form a righteous character by obedience to God's law. But he failed to do this, and because of his sin our natures are fallen, and we cannot make ourselves righteous." Steps to Christ, page 62.

Now notice, before the fall Adam could form a righteous character, but afterward his children could not because of their fallen nature. We are told repeatedly in the Spirit of Prophecy that Christ assumed a fallen nature. So, do you see that Adam and Christ were not equal in that sense. The question is, "Did Christ accept the law of heredity, as we must accept the law of heredity?" In the book, Questions on Doctrine, page 383, we are told by the authors (and I do not. know who the authors were)' that:

"(Christ) was exempt from the inherited passions and pollutions that corrupt the natural descendants of Adam. He was 'without sin, not only in His outward conduct, but in His very nature. Is this true? Was He exempt from the law of heredity? Sister White says that "He accepted the law of heredity: Like every child of Adam, He accepted the results of the working of the great law of heredity. What these results were is shown in the history of His earthly ancestors. He came with such a heredity to share our sorrows and temptations, and to give us the example of a sinless life." —Desire of Ages, page 49.

The brethren would have you believe He was exempt, but Sister White said he was not. Which view will you accept? I leave that with you and the Lord. Christ is called the second Adam. In purity and holiness, connected with God and beloved by God, He began where the first Adam began. Willingly He passed over the ground where Adam fell, and redeemed Adam's failure." --The Youth's Instructor, June 2, 1898.
Yes, He did begin where the first Adam began, but the question is, "Did He begin with the same perfect sinless nature, the same perfect moral worth and physical strength that Adam had?" No, he did not. Sister White says:

"It would have been an almost infinite humiliation for the Son of God to take man's nature, even when Adam stood in his innocence in Eden. But Jesus accepted humanity when the race had been weakened by four thousand years of sin." – Desire of Ages, page 49.

What am I trying to say? Am I saying that Adam was sinless and Christ was a sinner? Of course not. I'm saying that both the first and second

Adam were sinless as far as their minds were concerned. I'm saying that Jesus was not as strong as the first Adam. He was weakened physically, mentally, and morally. So, it was much more difficult for Christ than it was for the first Adam. I do not believe that there is anything in this statement that would imply that Christ did not inherit a sinful nature. He not only traveled over the ground where Adam lost the battle, but He must travel over my ground. He must travel over the ground that every human being must travel for He is an example for all created beings, not just Adam.

"He was to take his position at the head of humanity by taking the nature but not the sinfulness of man." Signs of the Times, May 29, 1901. (7A p. 447, QOD p. 651)

She says He took the nature. What nature? We are told by Mrs. White in Medical Ministry, page 181, "He took upon His sinless nature our sinful nature." So, there is no question as to whether or not He took the sinful nature. What is she saying? She is saying He took the sinful nature, but He did not accept the sinfulness of man. He never participated in Sin. He never accepted the clamorings of His flesh. He never allowed them to become the director of His life. He instantly through the power of the indwelling Holy Spirit rejected these temptations. So, in that sense, He did not take the sinfulness of man. She does not say here that He did not take the sinfulness of man's nature; but rather, He did not take the sinfulness of man "He vanquished Satan in the same nature over which in Eden Satan obtained the victory. The enemy was overcome by Christ in His human nature. "The Youth's Instructor, April 25, 1901. (7A p. 447, QOD p. 651)

Now notice, she does not say here that Christ did not take a sinful nature; but, rather, He overcame with the same nature that Adam had. She's not discussing sinful or sinless nature; she is discussing human nature in general. She is saying that Christ overcame the
devil in human nature. It is not a discussion of sin or sinlessness at all.

"In taking upon Himself man's nature in its fallen condition, Christ did not in the least participate in its sin." — S.D.A.B.C., Vol.5, page 1131. She's not saying here that Christ did not take a sinful nature; but, rather, He did not participate in the sin which was in the fallen nature. Again, I emphasize the little three-letter word "its." The "its" refers back to the nature. Let me paraphrase this statement. In taking upon Himself man's sinful nature, Christ did not participate in the sin that was in that nature.

"Could Satan in the least particular have tempted Christ to sin, He would have bruised the Savior's head. As it was, he could only touch His heel. Had the head of Christ been touched, the hope of the human race would have perished." — The SDA Bible Commentary, Vol. 5, page 1131.

Again, I believe that Mrs. White is saying here that Christ had a perfect, holy, spotless character, and it was never touched by the devil. The head of Christ was never touched, but the heel which represents the flesh, the lower nature was. Here is where the old devil works.

I do not believe that the higher nature is in the brain and the lower nature is in my toes. I don't believe that for a moment. I believe all sin takes place in the mind, but I do believe that there is a higher portion of the brain and a lower section of the brain, and that all the nerve endings from the body are channeled to this lower portion of the brain. They all must go through the hypothalamus, which I believe is the switchboard of the soul. So, when I speak of the higher and lower nature, I'm speaking of a dichotomized mind.

I'm being facetious now, but the next time you stub your toe, try rubbing your brain to see if it helps. I think you'll find that you'll get a lot more satisfaction by rubbing your toe. I realize that without the brain you would have no pain, but there is this sensation that goes to the brain where it is registered and defined as pain. When a mosquito lands on your arm and starts biting, you don't slap your brain, you slap the mosquito.

There are these impulses coming at you, and the brain must decide what it's going to do. The hand does not automatically hit the mosquito. This is not just a neuromuscular response; there must be a choice made. So again, when I speak of higher and lower nature, please understand it in this light.

"Be careful, exceedingly careful as to how you dwell upon the human nature of Christ. Do not set Him before the people as a man with the propensities of sin. He is the second Adam. The first Adam was created a pure, sinless being, without a taint of sin upon him." (7A p 447, QOD, p. 651)

"He took upon Himself human nature, and was tempted in all points as human nature is tempted. He could have sinned; He could have fallen, but not for one moment was there in Him an evil propensity. He was assailed with temptations in the wilderness, as Adam was assailed with temptations in Eden." The SDA Bible Commentary, Vol 5, page 1128.

Of all the statements in the Spirit of Prophecy, these two are used most often as proof Christ did not have sinful tendencies as we do. But, before we draw a hasty conclusion, let's take the word propensity as defined by Webster. He says it is natural inclination or tendency, a bent. Now if Christ had no natural tendencies, then He would not have responded to those in need the way He did. You see, there are not only evil tendencies but good tendencies as well. Now as far as Christ's mind was concerned, not for one moment was there in Him an evil propensity (tendency), but as far as the sinful nature that He took at birth, there were all the clamorings and tendencies that all human beings inherit. But remember, Christ never responded to an evil propensity (tendency), bent, or inclination because of the presence of the indwelling Holy Spirit.

According to Mrs. White, even after a person has been born again these tendencies must be kept in check or beat back.
"Paul was ever on the watch lest evil propensities should get the better of him. He guarded well his appetites and passions and evil propensities (Letter 27, 1906). SDABC, Vol 6, page 1089

Note, he guarded them Do you think she's saying that Paul was guarding the evil desires of his mind? I don't think so. The Scriptures tell us that "for as he thinketh in his heart (mind), so is he." Proverbs 23:7 For one to have an evil propensity (tendency) in his mind he would be a sinner. Christ never once had an evil propensity in His mind, so with Christ He never had to have these propensities cut away from His character as we must; but He did have to keep them beat back as all men do, or else He was not tempted in all points as I am. Remember now "He accepted the law of heredity" —Desire of Ages, page 49. "Self, self, will be continually active for recognition, even in the very holiest of exercises. "In Heavenly Places, page 220.

"In treating upon the humanity of Christ, you need to guard strenuously every assertion, lest your words be taken to mean more than they imply, and thus you lose or dim the clear perceptions of His humanity as combined with divinity. His birth was a miracle of God. (7A p. 448 QOD, pg 652

Never, in anyway, leave the slightest impression upon human minds that a taint of, or inclination to, corruption rested on Christ, or that He is in any way yielded to corruption." SDA Bible Commentary, Vol 5, Pg 1128.

The most important word is rested. In other words, even though Christ was tempted in all points as we are tempted, not for one moment did He ever cherish an evil thought. Satan suggests impure thoughts, but none of these impure thoughts ever rested upon Christ. The moment the thought came, it was instantly repelled; so, they did not rest, they found no lodging place in the mind of Christ.

"The incarnation of Christ has ever been, and will ever remain, a mystery." The SDA Bible Commentary, Vol. 5, page 1129. (7A p. 448, QOD p. 652)

Again, I emphasize, it is not the nature that Mrs. White is talking about. She does not say that the nature which He assumed is a mystery, but rather how did God become a human being. That will always remain a mystery.

"That which is revealed, is for us and our children, but let every human be warned from the ground of making Christ altogether human, such as one as ourselves; for it cannot be." Ibid.

I do not believe that Christ was exactly like me, but He still inherited the same sinful nature. He had all the weaknesses upon Him, but not once did He ever sin, and so, therefore, He had no guilt of His own; but, rather, He bore the guilt of all of us. He never sinned in thought, deed, word or action; so, therefore He is not exactly as I am. But, in no way is Mrs. White saying here that He took a sinless nature. Again, the only way these statements could be saying this is if we read something into them that is not really there. I do not believe that these statements imply in any way, shape, or fashion that Christ assumed a sinless nature, as the authors of Questions on Doctrine would have you believe.

"He assumed the liabilities of human nature." The Signs of the Times, August 2, 1905. (7A p. 449, QOD, pg. 653)

"Christ bore the sins and infirmities of the race as they existed when He came to the earth to help man. In behalf of the race, with the weaknesses of fallen man upon Him…" The Review and Herald, July 28, 1874.

"Christ bore the sins and infirmities of the race as they existed when He came to the earth." Most people will admit that Christ bore the infirmities, but wait a minute. Sister White says Christ bore the sins and the infirmities of the race as they existed when He came. When did He come? Did He come as a full-grown man in A. D. 27? Or did He come as a babe in Bethlehem? He came as a babe in Bethlehem, didn't He? Therefore, that was the time that He inherited the infirmities and the sins of His forefathers. Remembering at all times that Jesus accepted the law of heredity; He was not exempt. - Desire of Ages, page 49.

"Jesus was in all things made like unto His brethren. He became flesh, even as we are." Desire of Ages, page 311. (7A p. 449, QOD p. 653)

The question is "What type of flesh do you have? Do you have sinful flesh or sinless flesh?" Remember now Mrs. White says not a soul has sinless flesh, for indeed, it is an impossibility. Let's read the whole quote.

"The teaching given in regard to what is termed "holy Flesh" is an error. All may now obtain holy hearts, but it is not correct to claim in this life to have holy flesh. The apostle Paul declares, "I know that in me (that is, in my flesh,) dwelleth no good thing' (Romans 7:18). To those who have tried so hard to obtain by faith so-called holy flesh, I would say, you cannot obtain it. Not a soul of you has holy flesh now. No human being on the earth has holy flesh. It is an impossibility." 2 Selected Messages, page 32.

Brothers and Sisters, how could I present to you a statement any clearer than that? No one has holy flesh, it's an impossibility. Even if you claim to have holy flesh by faith, she says "it is an impossibility." So, if man does not have holy flesh, what kind of flesh does he have? He has sinful flesh. How long will he have sinful flesh? Mrs. White says: "When human beings receive holy flesh, they will not remain on the earth, but will be taken to heaven. While sin is forgiven in this life, its results are not now wholly removed. It is at His coming that Christ is to 'change our vile body, that it may be fashioned like unto his glorious body' (Phil. 3:21) Ibid., page 33.

So, you see, we will retain the vile, corrupt, sinful flesh, or body right up to the second coming. But, remember the flesh of itself can't sin even though it's sinful. — Adventist Home, page 127. The mind must consent before one is actually termed a sinner, or he is held accountable for the sin. — Testimonies for the Church, Vol. 5, page 177.

I think the statement found in James 1:14,15   is quite clear on this subject:

"But every man is tempted, when he is drawn away of his own lust, and enticed. "Now notice, he didn't say that every man sins when he is drawn away of his own lust. No, it says in verse 15: "Then when lust hath conceived, it bringeth forth sin; and sin, when it is finished, bringeth forth death."

So, you see, it is not a sin to be tempted. Holy angels can be tempted. The only one that I know of that can't be tempted is God. The Bible says, "for God cannot be tempted with evil, neither tempteth he any man:" (James 1:13). When man is drawn away of his own lust and enticed then he is tempted, but he does not have to give in to the lust that is in his flesh. Right here we find the definition of how man is tempted. He is tempted when he is drawn away of his own lust. Now how could Christ be tempted like me if He did not have any lustful temptations? There had to be the same lustful temptations in His flesh just like in my flesh in order for Him to be tempted exactly as I am tempted. Now remember, we are told in Hebrews 4:15 that Jesus "was in all points tempted like as we are.

"The human nature of Christ is likened to ours, and suffering was more keenly felt by Him; for His spiritual nature was free from every taint of sin. The Signs of the Times, December 9, 1897 7A pg. 449 QOD pg. 653.

His spiritual nature - that nature that He received by faith was free from the taint of sin. Christ had three natures. He inherited the sinful nature of man, He had His own divine nature which He never used, and He also was a partaker of the divine nature by faith. Man has only two. Christ never used His divine nature to overcome sin. He Always relied upon the nature of His father which was given to Him by the Holy Spirit. He accepted it by faith. WE are told in the Spirit of Prophecy that Christ "could only keep the commandments of God in the same way that humanity can keep them (MS 1, 1892)—The SDA Bible Commentary, Vol 7, pg. 929.

"The Sinless One must feel the shame of sin…. Every sin, every discord, every defiling lust that transgression had brought, was torture to His spirit." The Desire of Ages, page 111. 7A pg. 450 QOD, p. 654.

"He realized the strength of indulged appetite and of unholy passion that controlled the world." Review and Herald, August 4, 1874. (7A p. 450, QOD, p. 654.
Now I ask you, how could Christ experience the effects of indulged appetite or feel the shame of sin from an external standpoint? You see, many people think that Christ was tempted only externally, that there was no internal strife whatsoever. This is a deception. Christ was tempted inwardly and outwardly. Mrs. white says:

"Christ was put to the closest test, requiring the strength of all His faculties to resist the inclination when In danger, to use His power to deliver Himself from peril, and triumph over the power of the prince of darkness." -The SDA Bible Commentary, Vol. 7, page 930.

Now that is an internal temptation, isn't it?
"The guilt of every sin pressed its weight upon the divine soul of the world's Redeemer." The Signs of the Times, December 5, 1892, 7A pg. 450, QOD pg.654.

"He took upon His sinless nature (His divine nature which He had from all eternity) our sinful nature (which He received from His mother), that He might know how to succor those that are tempted." Medical Ministry, page 181.

Can anyone find a statement any clearer than that?
In John 14:30, we are told:

"Hereafter I will not talk much with you: for the prince of this world cometh and hath nothing in me."

Does that mean that Jesus did not take a sinful nature? No....the prince of this world cometh, and hath nothing in me'—nothing to respond to temptation. On not one occasion was there a response to his manifold temptations. Not once did Christ step on Satan's ground, to give him any advantage. Satan found nothing in Him to encourage his advances. (Letter 8, 1895)." S.D.A.B.C., Vol 5, pg. 1129.

Again, Mrs. White is not saying that Christ did not take sinful flesh, but, rather, there was nothing in His mind that responded to these temptations.

"But the prince of darkness found nothing in Him; not a single thought or feeling responded to temptation." Testimonies, Vol 5, page 422. (7A p 450-451, QOD, p. 654-655)

"While He was free from the taint of sin, the refined sensibilities of His holy nature rendered contact with evil unspeakably painful to Him." The Review and Herald, Nov. 8, 1887.

Free from the taint of sin, again, no taint upon His character, none whatsoever, "Not even by a thought could Christ be brought to yield to the power of temptation." Ibid.

She is not saying that Christ was never tempted by an evil thought; but, rather, He never yielded even by a thought to the power of Satan.

This next statement is used quite often to discourage people from getting involved in the study of the Incarnation of Christ. She says:

"I perceive that there is a danger in approaching subjects which dwell on the humanity of the Son of the infinite God. He did humble Himself when He saw He was in fashion as a man, that He might understand the force of all temptations wherewith man is beset.... On not one occasion was there a response to his manifold temptations." The SDA Bible Commentary, Vol 5, page 1129.

She is not saying that we should not study it; but, rather, there is a danger in dwelling upon just the human side of Christ. He was also divine. This statement should not be interpreted to mean that we should not study this subject because we are told that the study of the nature of Christ, or the humanity of Christ, is a "fruitful field." She says "this is to be our study," as I have pointed out earlier in this thought paper.

The next statement is from Desire of Ages, page 49. I'm only going to comment on the latter part of the verse because I've previously commented on the first portion of this statement. But, this, I believe, is the most profound statement in all of the Spirit of prophecy on the subject of the nature of Christ.

"He (God) permitted Him to meet life's peril in common with every human soul, to fight the battles as every child of humanity must fight it, at the risk of failure and eternal loss."

Do we have a more trying conflict than Christ had? No. Was His conflict different than mine? No. It was the same conflict. He met man right where man is. "...Christ was to redeem Adam's failure. But when Adam was assailed by the tempter, none of the effects of sin were upon him...It was not thus with Jesus when He entered the wilderness to cope with Satan. For four thousand years the race had been decreasing in physical strength, in mental power, and in moral worth;and Christ took upon Him the infirmities of degenerate humanity. Only thus could He rescue man from the lowest depths of his degradation.:" Desire of Ages, page 117. (7A p. 452, QOD p. 656)

Notice—above "infirmities of degenerate humanity."

"Clad in the vestments of humanity, the Son of God came down to the level of those He wishes to save. In Him was no guile or sinfulness; He was ever pure and undefiled; yet took upon Him our sinful nature." The Review and Herald, December 15, 1896. Ibid. p. 453, PG 657.

Remember now, she says there was "no guile or sinfulness" And yet she says that "He took our sinful nature." Again, I say we must make the distinction between the higher and lower nature. "(he) became like one of us except in sin." Ibid. The Youth's Instructor, Oct. 20, 1886.

"He was born without a taint of sin, but came into the world in like manner as the human family." — Letter 97, 1898. 7A pg.453 QOD pg.657

How does the human family come into the world? — With a sinless nature, or with a sinful nature? The answer is obvious — a sinful nature. So, He came into the human race just like we do; yet, He had a perfect mind. The Holy Spirit was in His mind from birth.

"Christ, who knew not the least taint of sin or defilement, took our nature in its deteriorated condition. . . . What a subject for thought, for deep, earnest contemplation! . . . He stooped to poverty and to the deepest abasement among men." The Signs of the Times, June 9, 1898.

"Notwithstanding that the sins of a guilty world were laid upon Christ, notwithstanding the humiliation of taking upon Himself our fallen nature, the voice from heaven declared Him to be the Son of the Eternal." — Desire of Ages, page 112.

"Though He had no taint of sin upon His character, yet He condescended to connect our fallen human nature with His divinity. By thus taking humanity He honored humanity. Having taken our fallen nature, He showed what it might become, by accepting the ample provision He has made for it, and by becoming partaker of the divine nature." – Special Instruction Relating to the Review and Herald Office, and the Work in Battle Creek, May 26, 1896, page 13.

Here again, is a clear statement that Christ had a holy, perfect character, yet, He took, the fallen nature of man. Sister White emphasizes this in another place: "He was not only made flesh, but He was made in the likeness of sinful flesh. His divine attributes were withheld from relieving His soul anguish or His bodily pains (Letter 106, 1896)." The SDA Bible Commentary, Vol 5, page 1124.

Mrs. White was not confused at all as to what is meant in Romans 8:3. She says it was not just flesh, it was sinful flesh that He took

"In Christ were united the divine and the human — the Creator and the creature. The nature of God, whose law had been transgressed, and the nature of Adam, the transgressor, meet in Jesus — the Son of God. . ." (MS 141, 1901). The SDA Bible Commentary, Vol. 7, page 926.

Notice "the nature of God," the lawgiver, and "the nature of Adam, the transgressor, meet in Jesus. Now what type of nature does a transgressor have? It's a sinful nature. There is no other answer.

"We should have no misgivings in regard to the perfect sinlessness of the human nature of Christ." •The Signs of the Times, June 9, 1898 7A pg. 454 QOD pg.658.

Again, as I have stated over, and over again, Christ took our nature, but He didn't give in to it. She is not saying that He took sinless flesh, or a sinless nature. She is saying that Christ lived a sinless life in that sinful flesh. Just like the Bible tells us in Romans 8:3, Christ "condemned sin in the flesh." In whose flesh? In His flesh. He didn't sit back on a throne somewhere pointing His finger at sin and saying "you naughty, nasty thing." No, He condemned the sin that was in His own flesh. He never allowed it to become His master, rather He was the master of it. I say "He", He by faith because He says I of myself can do nothing. —John 5:30.

The following statement is used quite often to "prove" that Christ did not inherit a sinful nature: "He was a mighty petitioner, not possessing the passions of our human, fallen natures, but compassed with like infirmities, tempted in all points like as we are." Testimonies, Vol 2, page 508.

I do not believe that Christ had "like" passions, but I do believe that He had all the passions of our human nature. What do I mean by this? What I mean is this. The passions and lust that were in His flesh never became the dominating factor in His life. So, therefore, the passions that He had were not like mine because I have allowed the passions to control me. He never did; so, therefore, He did not have "like passions," as we have.

"Though He had all the strength of passion of humanity, never did He yield to temptation to do one single act which was not pure and elevating and ennobling." - In Heavenly Places, page 155. (Undated MS #73) He had all the strength of passion, but He never gave in to it. This is the secret.

"He is a brother in our infirmities, but not in possessing like passions." — Testimonies, Vol. 2, page 202.

The most important word is "like" passions, and again, I have explained what I believe that means.

"It was necessary for Him to be constantly on guard in order to preserve His purity. He was subject to all the conflicts which we have to meet, that He might be an example to us in childhood, youth, and manhood." Desire of Ages, page 71.

Subject to all the conflicts. Do you have internal conflicts? So did He.

This next statement I've commented on before, but I want to do it again. It is found in Signs of the Times, June 9, 1898.

"In taking upon Himself man's nature in its fallen condition, Christ did not in the least participate in its sin."

Again, the "its" refers back to the fallen nature. He took the fallen nature with the sin in it, but He did not participate in the sin which was in that nature. "He was without spot or blemish. "— The Spirit of Prophecy, Vol. 2, page 11,12.

His mind was "without spot or blemish," but the "heal," or the flesh, was defiled by sin. In Isaiah 53:12, we are told "he was numbered with the transgressors;" and in Hebrews 7:26, we are told "he was separate from sinners." Does the Bible contradict itself? No. The Lord is telling us that He met life's battle in common with every sinner, but He never gave in to His hereditary weaknesses. He was separate in that He never sinned. "(Christ will) forever. . .retain His human nature." - Desire of Ages, Page 25.

Some have used the argument that since Christ took this same human nature into heaven, it must have been a holy, perfect, sinless nature that He inherited from His mother because He has that same nature today in heaven. I do not believe that Christ came forth from the grave with the same elements He went into the grave with. I believe that Christ came forth from the grave with a body made of a finer material, yet it was a body that could be recognized. It had the nail prints in it and all, yet through the power of God, there was a change—a change in that body like we will be changed in a moment; but yet we will be recognized throughout eternity by our brothers and sisters. I can't explain how this takes place, but I do know that if Christ were to have lived on the earth and decided not to go through with the plan of salvation, He would have grown old and died. His flesh would have wrinkled like all of us. Why? Why would the flesh of Christ get wrinkled and die? If He had no sin in that flesh, there would have been nothing in it that would cause it to deteriorate. So, there had to be something in it which caused the flesh to wrinkle and deteriorate.

 According to Sister White, when we are resurrected:
"A much finer material will compose the human body, for it is a new creation, a new birth. It is sown a natural body, it is raised a spiritual body (Ms 76, 1900)." The SDA Bible Commentary, Vol. 6, page 1093.

I believe that Christ came forth from the grave with a glorified body, as we will.

The belief that Christ came to this earth and inherited a sinful nature with all the genetic disadvantages is not a new teaching; but, rather, it is the "historic" position of this church. According to Kenneth H. Wood, editor of the Review and Herald, the Christ of historic Adventism was a Christ who was tempted as we are tempted in all points, inwardly and outwardly. —Review and Herald, May 5, 1977.

What have I tried to convey in this thought paper? Simply this, Christ came to this world two thousand years ago, was born of a virgin, filled with the Holy Ghost. From the moment He was born until the time that He gave His life on the Cross, He was holy, undefiled, spotless, pure. Not once did He ever sin in thought, deed, word, or action; but at the same time, He inherited the same genetic disadvantages that every human being accepts when he comes into this life. The difference between Christ and us is that He was born filled with the Holy Ghost. We are not. That does not mean that it is an impossibility, but it's the exception rather than the rule. One exception mentioned in the Bible is John the Baptist.

I believe that Christ was different from us only in that He never sinned, and He had His own divinity which human beings do not have. Therefore, we cannot say that He was altogether man as we are. But, other than that, He was like us in all respects; but let us remember at all times that He never once used His divinity, not even to work a miracle. According to Mrs. White, Christ never worked a miracle: It was the angels of God that worked the miracles—Desire of Ages pages 92 and 143.

While on the one side He was totally divine, on the other side, He was made flesh, John 1:14, and Hebrews 2:14. There is only one flesh and blood known to humanity—that is sinful flesh and blood. He was made under the curse of the law. Galatians 4:4. This cannot mean that He was born under the ceremonial system, because the next verse says that He came to redeem them that were under the law. Now does that mean that He came to redeem the Jews only? Well, of course not. So, you can see that under the law means that He was under the curse of the law like every one of us is under the curse of the law. He was made to be a curse, Galatians 3:13. "The Lord hath laid on Him the iniquity of us all." --Isaiah 53:6. God hath made Him to be sin, 2 Cor. 5:21. "Who his own self bare our sins in his own body on the tree." Note: "in His body."—1 Peter 2:24.

Some have expressed the view that Christ never, in any real sense, experienced the temptations of man until He entered the Garden of Gethsemane, and it was at this time that God imputed the sinful nature of man to Christ. I cannot accept this concept since it bypasses the law of heredity. The nature that Christ took was not imputed in the Garden of Gethsemane; but, rather, it was inherited from His mother, Mary. Christ was tempted with that nature from the cradle to the cross, and not just in the Garden of Gethsemane. However, I do believe that His experience in the Garden was of real significance since He was beginning to realize how the sinner who rejects God's mercy will feel when he is brought forth from the grave only to die again. In other words, Christ had to die the second death. The first steps toward the second death began in the Garden of Gethsemane and culminated on the cross. There He experienced total separation from His Father, which is the second death. Not that God was not present, for the Scriptures say: "God was in Christ, reconciling the world unto himself."—2 Cor. 5:19. The words of Jesus testify to this feeling of separation: "My God, my God, why hast thou forsaken me?" –Matt. 27:46.

I firmly believe that until we accept the Christ of "historic Adventism" we are never going to understand by experience what righteousness by faith really is.

Usually what follows the acceptance of the concept that Christ inherited a sinless nature is a Christ who is my **Substitute** only and not my **Example**. Since He did it all for me on the Cross, all I have to do is accept what He did; and out of appreciation for what He did, I will show my love for Him by doing good and abstaining from certain things, such as alcohol, cigarettes, unclean talk, and things of this nature; which is the Evangelical view of sanctification, not the historic position of this church.

Sanctification is a part of righteousness by faith, not works of appreciation. Christ is my justification and my sanctification — 1 Cor. 1:30. Sanctification is the work of Christ, not man. Sanctification is a work of a lifetime to maintain, not to attain. We are to be sanctified every day. As far as justification is concerned, I believe Pastor Robert Wieland (Robert Wieland is Pastor of the Chula Vista Seventh-day Adventist Church, Chula Vista, California), hit the nail squarely on the head with his explanation. He says it is forensic effective; that is, a person can't be justified if there has been no change in his life, yet it is free and available for all. It can't be earned.

The righteousness by faith that we as Seventh-day Adventists should be advocating is a message that far exceeds that of the reformers. We are not to build a fence around anyone's theology. Light is ever progressive. See Appendixes C and D.

According to Mrs. White: "Luther had a great work to do in reflecting to others the light which God had permitted to shine upon him; yet he did not receive all the light which was to be given to the world."—The Great Controversy, page 148.

One last point. The Bible says, "Thanks be to God, which gives us the victory."—1 Cor. 15:57. Brothers and sisters, do you understand what that victory was? If you do not, you are not going to ask Christ to give you that same victory. If He did not overcome inclinations and tendencies (including sexual tendencies) in the flesh (not in the mind), then how can you pray to Christ and ask Him to give you the victory? Do you see how important the nature of Christ is in relation to righteousness by faith?

Remember, we are told by Mrs. White that in order to keep the Sabbath holy, men must themselves be holy. If we do not believe that we can be holy, by this I mean spotless with no desire to sin, no inclination or tendency in our mind to sin; if we do not believe that can be our experience, then the next step is if I can't be holy then I can't keep a holy day. And wouldn't the devil like to have you believe that.

At the beginning of this thought paper, I stated that there is controversy in the church on the subject of the nature of Christ and kindred topics, and I would like to close with a brief discussion as to whether or not it is wrong to enter into discussions of a controversial nature.

I firmly believe that if we, as Seventh-day Adventists are not united in our beliefs we cannot possibly go out and teach the world, so until we get it together, we really have no right to teach others. So, therefore, I have spent most of my energy in presenting the historic concept of the nature of Christ to our own people. I would like to ask the question, "Is it wrong to have controversy in the church?" Sister White says in Counsels to Writers and Editors, page 39:

"The fact that there is no controversy or agitation among God's people, should not be regarded as conclusive evidence that they are holding fast to sound doctrine. There is reason to fear that they may not be clearly discriminating between truth and error. When no new questions are started by investigation of the Scriptures, when no difference of opinion arises which will set men to searching the Bible for themselves, to make sure that they have the truth, there will be many now, as in ancient times, who will hold to tradition, and worship they know not what."
"God will arouse His people; if other means fail, heresies will come in among them, which will sift them, separating the chaff from the wheat."
--Ibid, page 40.

"Agitate, agitate, agitate! The subjects which we present to the world must be to us a living reality."—Ibid.

Selected Messages, Book 1, page 411:

"We are on dangerous ground when we cannot meet together like Christians, and courteously examine controverted points. I feel like fleeing from the place lest I receive the mold of those who cannot candidly investigate the doctrines of the Bible. Those who cannot impartially examine the evidences of a position that differs from theirs, are not fit to teach in any department of God's cause. What we need is the baptism of the Holy Spirit. Without this, we are no more fitted to go forth to the world than were the disciples after the crucifixion of their Lord. Jesus knew their destitution, and told them to tarry in Jerusalem until they should be endowed with power from on high."

Should we stand firm for the doctrines that we have held as a people for all these years? Councils to Writers and Editors, page 52:

"He calls upon us to hold firmly, with the grip of faith, to the fundamental principles that are based upon unquestionable authority." Special Testimonies, Series B, No.2, page 59. (1904)

"The lapse of time has not lessened their value." Special Testimonies, Series B, No. 2, page 41. (1904).

"No line of truth that has been made the Seventh-day Adventist people what they are, is to be weakened. We have the old landmarks of truth, experience, and duty, and we are to stand firmly in defense of our principles, in full view of the world." Testimonies, Vol. 6, page 17.
Councils to Writers and Editors, page 53:

"I saw a company who stood well-guarded and firm, giving no countenance to those who would unsettle the established faith of the body. God looked upon them with approbation. I was shown three steps, - the first, second, and third angels' messages. Said my accompanying angel, "Woe to him who shall move a block or stir a pin of these messages'". –Early Writings, pages 258, 259. (1858).

"In the future, deception of every kind is to arise, and we want solid ground for our feet. We want solid pillars for the building. Not one pin is to be removed from that which the Lord has established. The enemy will bring in false theories, such as the doctrine that there is no sanctuary. This is one of the points on which there will be a departing from the faith. Where shall we find safety unless it be in the truths that the Lord has been giving for the last fifty years?"—Review and Herald, May 24, 1905.

Counsels to Writers and Editors, page 56:

"There are occasions where their glaring misrepresentations will have to be met. When this is the case, it should be done promptly and briefly, and we should then pass on to our work. The plan of Christ's teaching should be ours. He was plain and simple, striking directly at the root of the matter, and the minds of all were met." --Testimonies, Vol. 3, page 37. (1872).

Is it safe for me to take a neutral position?

"If a brother is teaching error, those who are in responsible positions ought to know it; and if he is teaching truth, they ought to take their stand at his side. We should all know what is being taught among us; for if it is truth, we need to know it. We are all under obligation to God to understand what He sends us." Testimonies to Ministers, page 110.

"There is no such thing now as a neutral position. We are all decidedly for the right or decidedly with the wrong."   --Testimonies, Vol. 3, page 328.

"Indifference and neutrality in a religious crisis is regarded of God as a grievous crime and equal to the very worst type of hostility against God."—Testimonies, Vol. 3, page 281.
Brothers and sisters, I believe that this new view of the nature of Christ, which in fact is the Catholic concept, is a very dangerous, soul-destroying doctrine. It is the acceptance of this and other views that are being agitated among us as a people today that will lead us closer and closer to the borders of Egypt. Sister White says in Testimonies, Vol. 5, page 217:
The church has turned her back from following Christ her Leader and is steadily retreating toward Egypt." Again, she says in Signs of the Times, February 19, 1894: "It is the rejection of Bible truth which makes men approach to infidelity. It is a backsliding church that lessens the distance between itself and the papacy."

In closing, I would like to suggest that every one of you who takes the time to read this little book will also take time to restudy the message that was brought to this church in 1888. While Jones and Waggoner were the ones who presented it, it was a message from the Lord.

"The Lord in His great mercy sent a most precious message to His people through Elders Waggoner and Jones."—Testimonies to Ministers, page 91.
Note— "Message" is singular. We cannot accept Waggoner to the exclusion of Jones, or vice versa, because they presented one message.

It's a sad commentary that whenever you ask someone about the 1888 message, all too often the response is directed toward the apostasy of Jones and Waggoner rather than the message. I feel it's the same today as it was back in 1889 when Mrs. White said:

"There is not one in one hundred who understands for himself the Bible truth on this subject (justification by faith) that is so necessary to present and eternal welfare."—Review and Herald, September 3, 1889.

While it is true that Jones and Waggoner eventually apostatized, Sister White cautioned:

"It is quite possible that Elder Jones or Waggoner may be overthrown by temptations of the enemy; but if they should be, this would not prove that they had no message from God, or that the work that they had done was all a mistake. But should this happen, how many would take this position, and enter into a fatal delusion, because they are not under the control of the Spirit of God...I know that this is the very position many would take if either of these men were to fall, and I pray that these men upon whom God has laid the burden of a solemn work, may be able to give the trumpet a certain sound, and honor God at every step, and that their path at every step may grow brighter until the close of time. (Letter S-24, 1892).

It would be well to remember that the apostasy of these men took place long after the 1888 Conference. According to A.V. Olson in his book, Through Crisis to Victory," page 304, A.T. Jones was elevated to the position of leading editor of the Review and Herald on October 4, 1897. On page 305, of the same book, Olson states that Jones was elected as a member of the General Conference Committee the same year.

He also states of page 315 that it was 1906 when Wagoner was terminated from the church.

Mrs. White says:

"Should the Lord's messengers, after standing manfully for the truth for a time, fall under temptation and dishonor Him who has given them their work, will not be proof that the message is not true? No. Sin on the part of the messenger of God would cause Satan to rejoice, and those who have rejected the message and the messenger would triumph; but it would not at all clear the men who are guilty of rejecting the message of God..." (Letter 0 19, 1892).

How did Mrs. White respond to the message of Jones and Waggoner?

"I have had the question asked, What do you think of this light that these men (Jones and Waggoner) are presenting? Why, I have been presenting it to you for the last forty-five years, the matchless charms of Christ---.... When Brother Waggoner brought out these ideas at Minneapolis, it was the first clear teaching on this subject from any human lips I had heard, excepting the conversations between myself and my husband. I have said it to myself, it is because God has presented it to me in vision that I see it so clearly, and they cannot see it because they have not had it presented to them as I have, and when another presented it, every fiber of my heart said Amen." ---(MS 5, 1889)

Note, the message of Jones and Waggoner was not a reemphasis of the Luther and Calvin concept, but rather, the righteousness by faith message that was taught by Christ and Paul.

While much more could be said on the nature of Christ and Righteousness by Faith, I feel that there is enough presented here to, at least, stimulate the thinking of those interested in these subjects.

I thank you for taking time to read this paper.

All Biblical references are from the King James Version, unless otherwise noted.

All Ellen G. White quotations can be found at www.WhiteEsate.org

The Following pages are additional references which are relative to the subject of the incarnation of Jesus Christ.

Sources that I believe present the same concept that
I have set forth in this thought paper:

Holy Bible, especially Isaiah 53, Romans 3, Galatians 4,
    Philippians 2, and Hebrews 2.

Ellen G. White, especially Desire of Ages, pages 49 and 117,
    and Medical Ministry, page 181.

E. J. Waggoner, Christ and His Righteousness, pages 26-27,
    Pacific Press Publishing Ass'n.; Reprint 1972.
    Mrs. White endorsed Waggoner's concept of Righteousness
    by Faith. According to Robert Wieland, there are over
    200 endorsements in Spirit of Prophecy. See Wieland's
    1888 Message Itself, for endorsements. LeRoy Froom in
    his book, Movement of Destiny, pages 189-201, states
    the 1888 message is contained in Waggoner's books,
    Christ and His Righteousness, Gospel in Creation, and
    Glad Tidings.

A. T. Jones, The Consecrated Way to Christian Perfection,
    Pacific Press Publishing Ass'n, 1905. Read the whole
    book.

A. T. Jones, comments in the 1895 General Conference Bulletin.

Bible Readings for the Home Circle, 1916 edition, page 174. -
    "Christ inherited the sinful nature with all of the
    tendencies." - That statement no longer appears in the
    new editions of the Bible Readings. Why? Who took
    it out? By whose permission?

The Sabbath School Lesson Quarterly, 1st Qtr. of 1921.
    I realize that you do not have this in your library,
    but I'm sure that if you wrote to the General Conference
    that this material could be made available for you.

The Review and Herald, Dec. 21, 1905, Editor, W. W. Prescott;
    Associate Editors, L. A. Smith and W. A. Spicer.

Carlyle B. Haynes, The Return of Our Lord, especially
    pages 66-67, by the Review and Herald, 1926.

M. L. Andreasen, The Book of Hebrews, Review and Herald, 1948.
    Note: comments on Hebrews the 2nd chapter.

M. C. Wilcox, Questions and Answers, Pacific Press Publishing
    Ass'n., 1911.

Herbert E. Douglass and Leo Van Dolson, Benchmark of Humanity,
    Southern Publishing Ass'n., especially the chapter,
    "God with Us," pages 25-55.

Arnold Wallenkampf, <u>New by the Spirit</u>, Pacific Press
    Publishing Ass'n., 1978, <u>page 29</u>.

Herbert E. Douglass's view in the book, <u>Perfection</u>, Southern
    Publishing Ass'n., 1975.
    I do not agree with the other portions of this book,
    with the exception of Maxwell, who comes very close.
    I would like to sit down and talk with him. It may
    be semantics.

Pastor Robert J. Wieland, <u>1888 Message Itself</u>, 1977.
    I feel that this book should be presented to the
    Church at large. I have read it and circulated
    it, and I have received a tremendous blessing from
    this book, one of the most comprehensive studies on
    the 1888 movement that I have ever seen.

*William H. Grotheer, <u>An Interpretive History of the
    Doctrine of the Incarnation as Taught by the
    Seventh-day Adventist Church</u>, October, 1972,
    published by the Adventist Laymen's Foundation
    of Mississippi, Inc., - the best manuscript I've
    read on the nature of Christ. This should be given
    wide circulation.

William H. Branson, <u>Drama of the Ages</u>, Southern Publishing
    Ass'n., 1950, pages 95-104.

The books by A. T. Jones and E. J. Waggoner may be obtained
from one or more of the following sources:

    Your local Adventist Book Center

    Hudson Publishing Ass'n.
    P. O. Box 408
    Baker, Oregon 97814

    Leaves-of-Autumn Books
    P. O. Box 440
    Payson, Arizona 85541

The book by William H. Grotheer, and other material by him
including the book, <u>In the Form of a Slave</u>, may be obtained
at the following address:

    Adventist Laymen's Foundation
    P. O. Box 178
    Lamar, Arkansas 72846

APPENDIX A

What About "Original Sin"?

A REVIEW reader asks what Seventh-day Adventists believe with respect to "original sin." We shall try to reply briefly.

"Original sin" is a technical theological term implying that each of Adam's descendants has inherited the guilt resulting from his first transgression, and that God holds every member of the human family equally guilty with him for it. The text usually cited in support of this theory is Romans 5:12: "Wherefore, as by one man sin entered into the world, and death by sin; and so death passed upon all men, for that all have sinned." Those who believe that Paul here teaches the "original sin" concept, point out that Adam was not only an individual, morally responsible on his own behalf, but also the corporate head of the entire human family. In fact, together with Eve, his wife, he *was* the entire human race. Therefore, in Adam the entire human race became guilty before God.

It must be noted, however, that the "original sin" concept is a philosophical deduction read into the text. The words of Paul do not state the "original sin" theory. We note, first, that the apostle here sets forth a series of contrasts. Adam and Christ are thus contrasted, each in his respective role: one opened the door to sin; the Other, to salvation. When Paul completes his antithesis in verse 15, he similarly places grace in contrast with sin. In verse 12, "death passed upon all men," and in verse 15, "grace . . . hath abounded unto many."

The first question to be answered is this, "By the word 'sin' does the apostle mean man's sinful nature, his universal tendency (since the Fall) to commit sin? Or does he mean the guilt, or moral responsibility that follows as a natural result of sinful acts committed? Now, death is the result of sin, as Paul specifically declares. But the reason he gives for the fact that "death passed upon all men" is, that "all have sinned." He does *not* say that death, the penalty for sin, passed upon all men because Adam had sinned. Each man is morally responsible for his own sins, not for those of Adam or anyone else. The fact is explicitly set forth at length in Ezekiel 18. Note particularly verse 20: "The soul that sinneth, it shall die. The son shall not bear the iniquity of the father, neither shall the father bear the iniquity of the son." In other words, a sinful nature can be inherited, but the moral responsibility cannot.

If the "original sin" theory be accepted—*if* moral guilt passed upon all men as a result of Adam's transgression—then by a parity of reasoning the grace of Christ should likewise pass upon all men as a result of Christ's gift, irrespective of their choice in the matter. Right here the theory breaks down, for in the first instance it denies the effective validity of personal choice and denies man's individual moral responsibility and accountability, whereas in the second it affirms this very fact. The theory is thus inherently inconsistent. The very fact that the grace of Christ "abounds" only to those who believe (see John 1:12, 13), requires as its corollary that guilt "abounds" only to those who have personally incurred it.

For these reasons Seventh-day Adventists do not accept the "original sin" theory.

R. F. C.

APPENDIX B

174   *BIBLE READINGS*

priest in things pertaining to God, to make reconciliation for the sins of the people." Verse 17.

NOTE.— In His humanity Christ partook of our sinful, fallen nature. If not, then He was not "made like unto His brethren," was not "in all points tempted like as we are," did not overcome as we have to overcome, and is not, therefore, the complete and perfect Saviour man needs and must have to be saved. The idea that Christ was born of an immaculate or sinless mother, inherited no tendencies to sin, and for this reason did not sin, removes Him from the realm of a fallen world, and from the very place where help is needed. On His human side, Christ inherited just what every child of Adam inherits,— a sinful nature. On the divine side, from His very conception He was begotten and born of the Spirit. And all this was done to place mankind on vantage-ground, and to demonstrate that *in the same way* every one who is "born of the Spirit" may gain like victories over sin in his own sinful flesh. Thus each one is to overcome *as Christ overcame*. Rev. 3:21. Without this birth there can be no victory over temptation, and no salvation from sin. John 3:3-7.

7. Where did God, in Christ, condemn sin, and gain the victory for us over temptation and sin?

"For what the law could not do, in that it was weak through the flesh, God sending His own Son in the likeness of sinful flesh, and for sin, *condemned sin in the flesh*." Rom. 8:3.

NOTE.— God, in Christ, condemned sin, not by pronouncing against it merely as a judge sitting on the judgment-seat, but by coming and living *in the flesh, in sinful flesh*, and yet without sinning. In Christ, He demonstrated that it is possible, by His grace and power, to resist temptation, overcome sin, and *live a sinless life in sinful flesh*.

8. By whose power did Christ live the perfect life?

"I can of Mine own self do nothing." John 5:30. "The words that I speak unto you I speak not of Myself: but *the Father that dwelleth in Me, He doeth the works*." John 14:10.

NOTE.— In His humanity Christ was as dependent upon divine power to do the works of God as is any man to do the same thing. He employed no means to live a holy life that are not available to every human being. Through Him, every one may have God dwelling in him and working in him "to *will* and to *do* of His good pleasure." 1 John 4:15; Phil. 2:13.

9. What unselfish purpose did Jesus ever have before Him?

"For I came down from heaven, *not to do Mine own will, but the will of Him that sent Me*." John 6:38.

HAVE I need of aught, O Saviour!
    Aught on earth but Thee?
Have I any in the heavens,
    Any one but Thee?

Though I have of friends so many,
    Love, and gold, and health,
If I have not Thee, my Saviour,
    Hold I any wealth?

                CORIE F. DAVIS

APPENDIX C

There are different concepts of righteousness by faith now being advocated among us as a people, and some non-Adventist theologians are now having an impact on the thinking of many of our people, including the ministry. The cautions given in Appendix C and Appendix D by Robert H. Pierson and Mrs. White respectively, should be given earnest consideration in view of these various concepts. Elder Pierson cautions:

> "Already, brethren and sisters, there are subtle forces that are beginning to stir. Regrettably there are those in the church who belittle the inspiration of the total Bible, who scorn the first 11 chapters of Genesis, who question the Spirit of Prophecy's short chronology of the age of the earth, and who subtly and not so subtly attack the Spirit of Prophecy. There are some who point to the reformers and contemporary theologians as a source and the norm for Seventh-day Adventist doctrine. There are those who allegedly are tired of the hackneyed phrases of Adventism. There are those who wish to forget the standards of the church we love. There are those who covet and would court the favor of the evangelicals; those who would throw off the mantle of a peculiar people; and those who would go the way of the secular, materialistic world.
>
> Fellow leaders, beloved brethren and sisters-- don't let it happen! I appeal to you as earnestly as I know how this morning--don't let it happen! I appeal to Andrews University, to the Seminary, to Loma Linda University--don't let it happen! We are not Seventh-day Anglicans, not Seventh-day Lutherans--we are Seventh-day Adventists! This is God's last church with God's last message!"

The statements quoted above are taken from the article, "An Earnest Appeal from the Retiring President of the General Conference" by Robert H. Pierson, which appeared in the Adventist Review, October 26, 1978.

www.ingramcontent.com/pod-product-compliance
Lightning Source LLC
Chambersburg PA
CBHW051406150726
48000CB00003B/1352